W9-CMB-788

# DRUGS AND SLEEPING DISORDERS

Few people understand how important to your health getting enough sleep is.

THE DRUG ABUSE PREVENTION LIBRARY

# DRUGS AND SLEEPING DISORDERS

Gina Strazzabosco-Hayn

THE ROSEN PUBLISHING GROUP, INC.
NEW YORK

Published in 1996 by The Rosen Publishing Group, Inc.
29 East 21st Street, New York, NY  10010

Copyright 1996 by The Rosen Publishing Group, Inc.

All rights reserved. No part of this book may be repro-
duced in any form without permission in writing from
the publisher, except by a reviewer.

First Edition

**Library of Congress Cataloging-in-Publication Data**
Strazzabosco-Hayn, Gina.
    Drugs and sleeping disorders / Gina
Strazzabosco-Hayn.
        p.   cm. — (The Drug abuse prevention library)
    Includes bibliographical references and index.
    ISBN 0-8239-2144-1
    1. Sleep disorders—Juvenile literature.
    2. Substance abuse—Juvenile literature.  [1. Sleep
disorders.  2. Sleep.  3. Drug abuse.  4. Drugs.]
    I. Title.  II. Series.
    RC547.S77   1995
    616.8'498—dc20                                    95-13023
                                                            CIP
                                                             AC

*Manufactured in the United States of America*

# Contents

# Introduction

*O*ver fifty million people in North America have some sort of sleeping disorder. The disorders range from snoring to insomnia to sleep apnea, a condition in which the sufferer temporarily stops breathing while sleeping. There are many ways of coping with sleeping disorders; one of the most common, and most unfortunate, is with drugs.

Several over-the-counter and prescription drugs can help a person suffering from a sleeping disorder to sleep through the night. These are often the easiest methods of relief. However, what most people don't realize is that taking drugs to solve one problem often leads to a worse problem: addiction.

Your body needs a certain amount of sleep every night in order to function well.

Students often put off sleep to study or finish homework.

# CHAPTER 1

# Sleep Is More Important than You Think

*B*elieve it or not, sleeping is one of the most important things you can do for your health. Sleep is a biological function. When you sleep, your body rests and rejuvenates itself. It is as necessary to the body as food and drink.

The amount of sleep needed to feel well rested differs from person to person and lessens as you grow older. An infant may spend as many as 12 hours sleeping each day. The average adult needs eight hours. The elderly generally need only six. According to one study, the average teenager may need more than nine-and-a-half hours of sleep a night to maintain a healthy body and an alert mind.

10 | ## *Normal Sleep*

Sleep is a complex behavior. It occurs in two phases: NREM, nonrapid eye movement, and REM, rapid eye movement.

NREM sleep is broken into four stages that repeat in cycles during the night. The first, Stage 1, is a light sleep that occurs during the first few moments of sleep. This gradually moves into Stage 2, a slightly heavier sleep that may last between five and fifteen minutes. You briefly slip into Stage 3 sleep, and then move on to Stage 4, the deepest sleep, which may last for 20 to 40 minutes. Then the brain signals a change to REM sleep. This is when you begin to dream.

## *Everyone Dreams*

There are many theories on why people dream. The renowned psychoanalyst Dr. Sigmund Freud introduced the theory that dreaming was the way the brain worked through problems encountered while awake. Dr. Freud also believed that dreams allowed people to express desires or behavior that were socially unacceptable. Another famous psychoanalyst, Dr. Carl Jung, suggested that dreams remind us of the important parts of our personalities that we didn't use while awake. He

believed dreams keep us psychologically **11**
balanced. Others believe that dreams allow us to filter through the day's events,
storing the important experiences as
memories, forgetting the rest.

Research on the function of dreams
continues. For now, just keep in mind
that everybody dreams several times a
night.

### REM *Sleep*

Dreams occur during REM sleep. No one
is quite sure why our eyes move when we
dream. The most popular theory today is
that there is some connection between the
movements and the dreams. Because of
an effective block that your brain places
on your central nervous system when you
sleep, your body does not carry out the
actions portrayed in your dreams. The
rapid eye movements may be the body's
way of attempting to carry out at least
some of the actions of the dream.

Experts all seem to agree that REM
sleep is a vital function. Between 90 and
120 minutes of sleep per night is spent in
REM sleep. In fact, a person deprived of
REM sleep one night spends more time in
REM sleep the following night.

Despite science's inability to tell us

12 | exactly why sleep—particularly REM sleep—is important, the fact remains that a good night's sleep is essential to daily functions.

# CHAPTER 2

# What Are Sleeping Disorders?

*T*here are several kinds of sleeping disorders. The most common include the following.

### Sleep Deprivation

Few people are convinced that sleep is as necessary as the experts claim. In fact, most Americans are sleep-deprived, many because they choose to be. Our society has developed into a 24-hour society. People even like to boast about how little sleep they got the night before.

*"Man, am I tired! I went to bed at one a.m. and had to get up at six to catch the bus."*

**14**

*"At least you got five hours of sleep. I was up until three trying to do a project that's due today that I hadn't even started. My alarm went off at five so I could finish. I am wiped out."*

*"I didn't even get to bed last night. I was up half the night jamming to the new Green Day* CD. *Figured I might as well just stay up. I'm dying for a Coke, though."*

Most people cringe when they think of going to bed "early." "When will I get everything done?" they think. Teens get an average of seven hours of sleep a night. A teenager who rises at 7 a.m. must go to sleep at 10 p.m. to get the nine hours of sleep he probably needs to be well rested. Most teens haven't even begun their homework, made their nightly phone call to a boy- or girlfriend, or finished watching the show of the month by then, much less even thought about heading off to bed.

Nearly every student has crammed for a test or written a paper in one night at some point in his life. Cramming and speed-writing are usually done between the hours of midnight and 4 a.m., precisely the hours during which most people need to sleep. These are also the

Students usually cram for a test or try to write a paper due the next day between the hours of midnight and 4 a.m.

*16* hours when people claim to be the most creative. "I work best under pressure," many people insist. These people generally don't realize that keeping such hours only serves to decrease their ability to function well on a regular basis. A body cannot be deprived of food or water and be expected to work at all, much less at peak. Sleep is as necessary an element to the body as food or water.

In an effort to force their bodies to do their bidding, people often use drugs such as amphetamines (speed) or caffeine to help keep themselves awake. These always have a negative effect, if not immediately, then sometime down the road.

## Insomnia

About one third of Americans, and 12 to 14 percent of teenagers, suffer from insomnia, or difficulty falling or staying asleep. This disorder is usually temporary. It is often brought on by stress such as trouble at school or a family crisis. Sometimes, however, insomnia can last for months or even years. People faced with chronic, or long-term, insomnia often turn to sleeping drugs or alcohol to get the rest they desperately seek. The results are not what the sleepless person hopes for, but rather addiction to the drug.

*Marla always had trouble falling asleep. Every night she'd get into bed with a stack of magazines at her side because she knew it could take hours for her to feel tired enough to drop off. Then, when she had to wake up at 7 a.m. for school, she was exhausted. The sleepiness usually lasted well into fifth period. She actually received detention twice for falling asleep in class. One more time and she'd be kicked out of the school play. She had mentioned her insomnia to her parents, but her father didn't seem to care, and her mother told her to deal with it as best she could. Perhaps it would go away someday.*

*One evening Marla saw a commercial for Sominex, an over-the-counter sleeping pill. "Aha," she thought. "There's the answer. Take a couple of those babies and I'll be out in seconds. I'll finally be able to stay awake in Civics class." She stopped off at the drugstore the next day after school.*

*That night she pulled out the box with excitement. "Maybe I'll only need one mag to get me through tonight," she thought, as she popped out two pills. She swallowed them, hid the box from prying parental eyes, and climbed into bed. She didn't even get halfway*

Sleeping pills affect the quality of sleep you get as well as how you feel when you wake up.

*through her first magazine before she fell deeply asleep. Her light was still on when her alarm woke her the next morning.*

*"Oh, man. Already? They should ban alarm clocks. Better yet, they should start school at a normal hour, like ten o'clock." Marla dragged herself out of bed and into the shower. That morning, however, she was fully awake before she got on the bus. "This is great. Sleeping pills are the answer," she concluded.*

*Marla continued to take the pills for the next couple of weeks, but by the end of the second week, she realized that she needed to take more than the recommended two pills to* *get to sleep. So she took three. A week later she was taking four, and a month after that she was taking them with a swig of rum stolen from her parents. She had heard that alcohol would knock you right out. It did, but she had a hard time waking up the next morning. She began to feel even worse than she had when she wasn't sleeping enough. She was also irritated easily. She snapped at her friends and found that she couldn't pay attention in class. She nearly got thrown out of the play anyway because she picked a fight with the director, Mr. Meehan.*

*One afternoon, as she was straightening Marla's room, Marla's mother noticed the faint scent of alcohol in the glass she found on Marla's nightstand. Concerned, she took a quick peek under Marla's bed. She found three empty boxes marked "Sominex," and a half-empty bottle of rum she thought her husband had finished off. She had noticed a difference in Marla's behavior, but thought it was because of the usual insomnia. She had always had insomnia, too, and had learned to live with it. Of course, she always took naps during the day after she came home from her part-time job. She had figured that Marla would learn to deal with her insomnia as she grew older. Besides, Marla was young*

**20** *and healthy; she didn't need as much sleep as older people did. "I guess I should have taken Marla's complaints more seriously," she thought, fiddling with the empty boxes on the kitchen table, waiting for Marla to get home from school.*

## Sleepwalking

Sleepwalking, or somnambulism, is exactly what it sounds like: walking in your sleep. Sleepwalking is common, occurring in about 40 percent of all children, especially around the age of 11 or 12. Sleepwalking ranges from sitting up in bed and mumbling, to walking around the house, to actually walking outside. The sleepwalker, while truly asleep, appears to be awake. Although sleepwalking episodes are generally not harmful to the victim, he could end up in dangerous situations. There have been cases where a sleepwalker has fallen downstairs, opened a locked door and walked down the block, and even driven a car. They rarely even remember the incident.

## Snoring

Snoring is the loud noise some people make when they sleep. It is caused by the collapse of part of the throat during sleep.

The noise is made by the vibration of the
soft tissues at the back of the throat during the collapse. Everyone's muscles are
vulnerable to collapse while sleeping because the supporting muscles have no
tone or strength then. However, only
some people snore. Several factors con-
tribute to snoring:

- Obesity—The extra flesh can block
  the throat, thereby causing the
  noise.
- Drugs—Sleeping pills and even some
  cold medications often relax the
  muscles in the throat region, thereby
  causing snoring, or making it worse.
- Smoking—Smoking irritates the
  throat, which can also cause snoring.
- Stuffed nose—Some people snore
  when they have a cold, allergies, or
  hay fever.

Snoring can be extremely loud.
Normal speech is usually at approximately 40 decibels of loudness. A crying
baby or a radio is approximately 60 decibels. Snoring can reach 80 decibels, equal
to the loudness of some jackhammers.
Some snorers, or their bed partners, suffer from hearing loss.

## 22 | *Sleep Apnea*

People with sleep apnea, or obstructive sleep apnea syndrome, temporarily stop breathing while sleeping. From the Greek work *apnoia,* meaning "breathless," apnea means a lapse in breathing lasting longer than ten seconds.

It is estimated that between one and four percent of the American population suffer from this disorder. It is believed that sleep apnea is caused by an abnormally shaped airway. The shape of the airway is such that the natural flow of air into the body is blocked temporarily. There are two ways to tell if someone has sleep apnea: extremely loud snoring or a series of snorts followed by fairly long periods of silence. These lapses in breathing can happen up to a thousand times in a night. No wonder people with sleep apnea are usually exhausted during the day and often cannot help falling asleep.

The breathing lapses are not necessarily present every night. In fact, they usually appear only when the sufferer is sleeping on his back. Once the person is turned on his side, he generally begins to breathe normally again.

## Shift Work or Delayed Sleep-Phase Syndrome

Humans are diurnal, or programmed to sleep at night. Our societies generally reinforce that by expecting work during the day, recreation in the evening, and sleep at night. Those who do shift work, or work at what are deemed unusual hours, nearly 20 percent of the population of the United States, almost always suffer some sort of sleep disruption. Between the noisiness of life during the daytime hours when these people try to sleep, and their body's natural desire to be awake, shift workers often get an average of seven fewer hours of sleep a week than their day-time colleagues. They often complain of sleepiness at work and of disruptions during sleep.

Delayed sleep-phase syndrome (DSPS) is a disorder involving the timing of sleep. As mentioned above, most humans are designed to sleep at night. In fact, our natural body rhythms tell us to do so. However, these same rhythms in people with DSPS tell them to fall asleep much later. Therefore, efforts to fall asleep earlier are futile. Those who suffer from DSPS often cannot fall asleep earlier than 3 or 4 a.m. As a result, they cannot wake

24 | up before 10 or 11 a.m. This pattern can cause work or academic performance to suffer. People with DSPS often turn to sleeping pills or alcohol to gain sleep.

### Periodic Leg Movements Syndrome

Periodic leg movements syndrome (PLMS) is surprisingly common. As the name suggests, PLMS is the occasional movement of one's legs, feet, or toes during sleep. These movements repeat themselves at specific intervals throughout the night, generally every 20 or 40 seconds. Periodic leg movements are apparently triggered by a command in the brain, but no one knows quite what the trigger is or why it occurs. It is difficult to diagnose PLMS. A person who suffers from PLMS might complain of insomnia, excessive sleepiness during the day, or unrestful sleep. He may not know that his legs move throughout the night.

Periodic leg movements in sleep can be provoked by or associated with several different medications, including depressants. Conversely, PLMS is treated exclusively with prescribed medications.

### Narcolepsy

The word narcolepsy means "sleep sei-

Someone suffering from PMLS may not know his legs move throughout the night until he sees his covers scattered about the area.

zure." The concept of narcolepsy as a disorder means excessive daytime sleepiness. A person with narcolepsy experiences unwanted episodes of sleep during the day. This happens most often when the person is engaged in a sedentary activity, such as during a play, a concert, or a lecture. Sometimes, however, a person can drop off to sleep during monotonous, and potentially dangerous situations, such as while driving. People with narcolepsy have even been known to have a sleep attack while talking or eating.

26    It has been estimated that at least 250,000 people have narcolepsy in the United States. Narcolepsy generally appears during adolescence or young adulthood, between the ages of 15 and 35. Most people with narcolepsy feel refreshed if they take a 20- to 30-minute nap when feeling such extreme sleepiness. Some may nap for more than an hour.

Treatment for narcolepsy may include prescription medications along with teaching the importance of regular sleeping habits and the value of naps throughout the day.

Narcolepsy often begins during adolescence.

Many people who suffer from sleeping disorders turn to sleeping pills without understanding the possible consequences.

# CHAPTER 3

# Methods of Controlling Sleep

*T*here are a lot of sleep disorders. The most common, as you now know, is simply sleep-deprivation. As you may also know, from experience or from the commercials you see in the media, there are several ways to control your sleeping habits. Some help you stay awake; some help you sleep. Some are sold as over-the-counter drugs in your local pharmacy; others are prescribed by doctors. There are also illegal methods of controlling sleep. These include illicit drugs, alcohol (taken by anyone under the age of 21), or medication prescribed for someone else. We'll take a look at the pros and cons of each of these methods of coping with your body's needs.

## 30 | *Keeping Yourself Awake*

It is not difficult to keep yourself awake. It is also not healthy to keep your body working longer than it wants to. Some people use stimulants to keep going when they are tired. But stimulants have negative effects.

### *Legal Stimulants*

"Revive, with Vivarin!"

"Jolt Cola—All the sugar and twice the caffeine!"

"The best part of waking up is Folger's in your cup."

Do these ads sound familiar? They all advertise the same thing: forcing your body to wake up.

Products such as coffee, tea, certain sodas, and chocolate contain caffeine. Caffeine works by stimulating your central nervous system and speeding up your metabolism.

Many adults begin each day with a cup of coffee or tea. Some even believe they can't start their day without it. Teens often drink a caffeinated soda during the middle of the day to help them stay awake for classes or to gain energy for sports or other after-school events. Caffeine will certainly perk you up during the day, but it will also keep you up at night.

One cup of coffee has 100 to 150 milligrams (mg) of caffeine; an 8-ounce cup of tea, about 40 (mg); a 12-ounce cola, 35 to 40 mg; and a chocolate bar up to 25 mg. When caffeine is taken shortly before bed—a last cup of tea, a chocolate bar (or two) for dessert, or a couple of Cokes—it can keep you awake. It takes as little as 100 mg of caffeine to steal two hours from a potential eight-hour sleep. It takes longer to fall asleep when you have caffeine, and the sleep you actually get tends to be restless and broken up by brief awakenings. Fifty-three percent of people who drink small amounts of coffee after 7 p.m., and 22 percent of people who drink large amounts of coffee after 7 p.m., report attacks of insomnia.

If you are making an effort to avoid caffeine, be sure to read the label of any soda you are considering. A soda does not have to be dark to contain caffeine, as proven by the labels of Mountain Dew and Sunkist Orange soda. Likewise, some dark sodas, including root beer and cream soda, do not contain caffeine. Caffeine is not necessarily an ingredient naturally found in soda. Companies actu-

*32* | ally add to some soda the caffeine they extract while decaffeinating coffee and tea because they know caffeine is addictive and it will keep you buying their product.

Products such as Vivarin, No-Dōz, and coffee tablets are sold specifically to help you stay awake when your body wants to sleep. A person may use these products when studying for a test, baby-sitting, or driving on a long trip. These stimulants contain between 100 and 200 mg of caffeine, along with other stimulants. Students, truck drivers, and people who work the late shift are among those who take these stimulants. They help keep you alert for a while, but then they wear off. People often take them with a swig of whatever they are drinking, which is usually coffee or caffeinated soda. Those combinations increase the caffeine intake. It is easy to lose track of how much caffeine you've consumed when your mind is on the paper you are trying to finish or the destination you are trying to reach.

Most people know that caffeine is addictive. What most people don't realize is how little it takes to become addicted to it. All it takes is two cups of coffee, four cans of caffeinated soda, or four cups of tea a day to get you addicted. As with any

drug, once addicted, your body builds up |
a tolerance. That means that it takes
more and more of the drug—in this instance, caffeine—to get the same result
that a small amount once did. Whereas
one can of caffeinated soda might have
made you more alert last week, it takes
two or three now. One caffeine pill might
have helped you stay awake for three
hours last month. Now it takes two. Soon
it will take three or four.

Taking too many caffeine tablets or
drinking too much caffeine can lead to
caffeinism. Caffeinism, or the consump-
tion of more than 1,000 mg of caffeine a
day, can cause anxiety or panic attacks,
restlessness, nervousness, and high blood
pressure.

If you are addicted, and if you try to
go for a day or two without caffeine, you
will probably experience withdrawal
symptoms. That is because your body
craves the drug. When you deprive your
body of the drug you've trained it to
need, it reacts. You might have headaches,
distractedness, and daytime drowsiness
for as long as a week. But when the withdrawal symptoms do end, you will find
that you get a great night's sleep.

Caffeine is also found in some cold

*34* medicines, so it is wise to read the ingredients of any medication you take before going to bed. Since you know that caffeine just before bed will keep you awake, avoid taking a medication containing caffeine before trying to sleep.

## Illegal Stimulants

Like caffeine, illegal stimulants excite your system. They delay the onset of sleep, increase wakefulness, and seem to increase alertness. People sometimes use illegal stimulants to keep themselves awake and have energy to do activities such as schoolwork, work, or other activities. These drugs are also addictive. There are two kinds of addiction. *Physical* addiction means that your body craves the drug and cannot function without it. *Psychological* addiction means that your mind craves the effects the drug has on you. Either way, you begin to think only of the drug, when you can get the next hit, how you will pay for it, and how you will feel during the high. The two most common illegal stimulants are amphetamines and cocaine.

*Amphetamines*, also called "speed" or "uppers," are usually found in pill form and are sometimes prescribed for obese

In the end, illegal drugs only hurt your body. You do yourself a favor when you avoid them.

people to assist in losing weight. They are also sold on the street. When you use speed, you feel as though you have boundless energy. When you come down off your high, however, you are exhausted and have virtually no energy. Sleep, however, is elusive. (In fact, an addict's general health declines to such a point that if he doesn't stop taking the drugs, he could die.)

As a result, people who are addicted to speed often become addicted to barbiturates, or "downers," as well. As the name implies, downers sedate the body, allow-

36 | ing it to catch the sleep it desperately seeks. However, that sleep is rarely restful or restorative. An addict wakes up feeling tired and sluggish. To shake yourself out of it, you take some speed. That gets your system going almost too well. You reach for a downer again that night to sleep. And so the cycle perpetuates itself.

*Tonya spied her friends waiting outside the new dance club. They'd all been waiting for weeks for it to open.*

*Tonya had had a difficult week. Between exams and baby-sitting for her younger brother and sister nearly every night, she was exhausted. But she could hardly wait until Friday. She'd heard that Keith was going to the club that night, and she'd had her eye on him all year. She was going to dance with him if it killed her.*

*"Hey, Tonya," Simone greeted her. "We thought you'd never make it. We just saw Keith head inside." She gave Tonya a knowing look. "He's a babe."*

*"Yeah, let's go in," Tonya replied, leaning against the wall of the building.*

*"What's up, Tonya? You look wiped. You're never going to get Keith to dance with you if you're holding up a wall somewhere inside," Tameka nudged Tonya.*

*"I had a long week. But I'm ready to party. Let's go!" But her slumped shoulders belied her enthusiastic words.*

*"I've got something for you." Simone reached into her tiny pocketbook and pulled out a baggie with a few pills. "Try a couple of these. They'll give you enough energy to snag Keith, James, and Jose."*

*"What are those? I never saw you take those before."*

*"They're uppers, honey. They're my sister's. You know how she's always trying to lose weight? Well, her doctor finally gave her something to help. I took some 'cause they make me fly!" Simone tried her best, but she couldn't persuade Tonya to take the pills. Finally she said, "C'mon, Tonya. Don't be so weak. Just one." She held it out enticingly.*

*"Simone, I just don't want to take something that's meant for someone else. I'll get Keith to dance with me. Don't you worry about that. I just need to feel the beat of the music and see his fine body to get me high. Thanks, anyway." Pumped up by the mini confrontation, she turned to Tameka and said, "Let's go in!" They turned and headed for the door.*

*"Wait up!" Simone yelled, stuffing the baggie back inside her pocketbook without taking any of the pills.*

Cocaine is highly addictive and extremely destructive to your body.

*Cocaine* is sold in powder form and is usually snorted through the nose. Cocaine is highly addictive. People on cocaine generally become more alert, talkative, and are sometimes described as "hyper." Their heart rate increases, their blood pressure rises, and they seem to need little or no sleep.

In reality, everyone needs sleep. A cocaine user just gets less of it. If you are addicted to cocaine, you suffer not only from sleep deprivation, but from the direct effects of the drug. Cocaine speeds up your heartbeat and rate of breathing.

If you snort it, the inside of your nose dries out, cracks, and bleeds. The drug eventually eats a hole in the lining of your nose, and only surgery will fix it. You become thin because you don't feel hungry. You get headaches and your eyesight becomes blurry. You may find yourself vomiting and suffering from stomach cramps. Finally, you risk overdosing, taking too much of the drug at one time. When you are high, you don't pay attention to what you're putting into your body. You only care about the high that comes from it.

There is no quick cure for cocaine addiction. It is very difficult to recover from that addiction, but it is possible with professional help. You can find a list of sources at the back of this book.

A stronger, crystalline form of cocaine is called *crack*. It is smoked. Crack is immediately addictive. If you try it, you will become addicted to it. Its high lasts about ten minutes, and the crash is nearly unbearable. The world of a crack addict is small, consisting of the drug, the supplier, and the hardware to smoke. Sleep, food, clothing, warmth, and safety all take a back seat to the addict's immediate need to get high. Overdosing is a constant

40 threat, but not one that the addict worries about. Like cocaine, it is difficult to break crack's hold on an addict without professional help.

LSD, d-lysergic acid diethylamide, is a hallucinogenic drug. It is not necessarily considered a stimulant, but it does have a somewhat stimulating effect on your body. Usually taken in small doses called tabs, LSD produces hallucinogenic visions, or trips. Some are "good," some are bad. "Good" trips can include visions of beautiful colors and new understandings of everyday events; bad trips can make you feel as if you have bugs crawling under your skin or that a beast is after you. One big risk of using LSD is that you can have flashbacks of a bad trip years later.

Some studies suggest that LSD increases wakefulness and decreases overall REM sleep. Other studies suggest that LSD increases REM sleep at the beginning of the night but does not affect the total amount. Either way, LSD has some negative effect on your natural sleep pattern.

### Forcing Your Body to Sleep
While some people try to stay awake, others have trouble falling asleep. People with sleeping disorders, especially insom-

nia, often resort to drugs to get some rest. None of them are good for your body, but some are worse than others.

### Over-the-Counter Sleeping Pills

Over-the-counter (OTC) means that you can buy a medication without a doctor's prescription. According to a 1991 Gallup poll, 40 percent of people in the U.S. with insomnia medicate themselves with OTC sleeping pills, alcohol, or a combination of the two.

Sleeping pills such as Sominex or Nytol will put you to sleep for the night. However, they may also cause side effects the next morning. You may feel sluggish at first, almost as if you can't wake yourself up. You might also experience a dry mouth, dilated pupils, or an accelerated heart rate. You may have difficulty urinating, or you might even discover behavioral changes in yourself, such as irritability or a sense of distraction. Sleeping pills also have an effect on your short-term memory and your ability to learn new material.

Most doctors warn that sleeping pills should not be taken for longer than two to three weeks at a time. Some experts believe that your body builds up a toler-

*42* | ance to these pills, as with any drug, and you begin to need more and more of them to fall asleep. You could become dependent on sleeping pills; your body may not be able to fall asleep without them.

Most doctors agree that it is best to avoid using sleeping pills altogether. There are other methods of getting the sleep you need. These are discussed in Chapter 4.

### Prescription Sleeping Pills and Tranquilizers

Doctors may prescribe sleeping pills, or hypnotics, for someone who is temporarily suffering from a sleeping disorder (such as insomnia) because of a recent trauma (for instance, a death in the family). These are meant to be used for only a short time and should be used in conjunction with therapy or other methods of learning to deal with the traumatic situation.

Doctors also prescribe drugs called tranquilizers to help control unwanted behavior or feelings. Tranquilizers, the most frequently prescribed drugs during the 1980s, are usually prescribed to control anxiety disorders, including those that disturb a person's sleep. Although considered mild, tranquilizers do have side effects, including reduced alertness, loss of coordination, slurred speech, loss of memory, and unintentional and inappropriate sleep episodes. You can also become addicted to them. Once addicted, it is difficult to break free from their hold. Withdrawal symptoms can range from nightmares to convulsions.

If you have been prescribed sleeping pills or tranquilizers, it is important that you take them according to the doctor's instructions. Tranquilizers are safe when taken in the prescribed doses and for the indicated length of time. Do not take more than directed. Do not try to have the prescription refilled once it runs out. A doctor prescribes a certain amount of a drug for a reason. In the cases of sleeping pills and tranquilizers, it is because they are not effective or beneficial to you after two or three weeks. It is also important not to mix these drugs with alcohol. Mixing can lead to a coma or even death.

It is also dangerous to take pills that were prescribed for someone else. First, you don't know what they will do to your body. Second, you always run the risk of becoming addicted to them.

Caffeine and alcohol have opposite effects on your body. Caffeine is a stimulant, which keeps your body awake. Alcohol is a depressant, which slows your body down. Neither are good for your body.

### *Alcohol as a Sedative*

A sedative is something that relaxes you. All types of alcohol, from beer to wine coolers to whiskey, are depressants with sedative qualities. This means that alcohol depresses your system, thereby causing your body to relax. The specific method by which alcohol produces this sedative effect is not yet known. However, this has not stopped people suffering from sleeping disorders from turning to alcohol to help them sleep. This is a particularly dangerous method of inducing sleep, be-

cause most people who use alcohol for

this reason are taking other drugs to induce sleep, too. Mixing drugs and alcohol can be fatal.

Alcohol has an effect on daytime and nighttime behavior. While you are awake, alcohol can cause slurring, lack of coordination, nausea, vomiting, double vision, and dizziness. And, like other drugs, it can cause addiction. Alcoholism is a disease that will affect you for the rest of your life, whether you are a practicing or a recovering alcoholic.

While you are sleeping, alcohol keeps you from getting the proper amount of REM sleep. Knowing that each person needs a certain amount of REM sleep every night, you also know that eventually your body needs to catch up. If you continue to use alcohol, it never does. This can affect your temperament, causing you to feel anxious and irritated, as well as your attention span and concentration.

It is possible to recover from alcoholism. It is not easy, but organizations listed in the back of this book will put you in touch with people who can help.

## Barbiturates
Barbiturates, also known as "downers," are sedatives. They are found in the form

Sometimes people turn to alcohol to help them sleep. They don't realize that alcohol actually keeps them from sleeping well.

of pills and are often sold on the street to those looking to get high. Taken in large enough doses, they can induce sleep. Barbiturates are often used to counterbalance amphetamine abuse. In large enough doses, barbiturates can be fatal. They can also be fatal if taken with alcohol.

As with other drugs, the sleep that barbiturates induce is not restful. It does not allow you to get the REM sleep necessary to rejuvenate the body. It is also easy to become addicted to barbiturates. This addiction, like others, can be fought and conquered.

## Marijuana

Marijuana, commonly known as "pot," "weed," "grass," or "mary jane," is derived from the hemp plant. It is most often smoked, but it can also be eaten. It has mild sedative and hallucinogenic effects on the user. Marijuana is also addictive over a period of time. A person's body builds up a tolerance to marijuana rather quickly. The user needs more and more of the drug to get the same high that smoking one marijuana cigarette, or joint, achieved.

Studies have shown that marijuana increases the slow-wave sleep in a cycle of sleep. You spend more time in deep sleep and less time in REM sleep. When you awaken, you feel groggy and tired. In addition, withdrawal from the drug causes temporary sleeplessness and awakenings throughout the night. These effects do diminish once your body gets used to not having the drug.

## Heroin

Heroin, also called "smack," among other things, is a chemical substance derived from the opium poppy. Actor River Phoenix died of "multiple drug intoxication" including a deadly level of morphine,

**48** another derivative of the opium poppy.

Heroin is usually injected either under the skin (skin-popping) or directly into a vein (mainlining). Heroin is also sold in another form called "China White." China White is about 90 percent pure heroin, whereas a regular dose of heroin has a purity of about 5 to 10 percent. China White can be snorted or smoked just like cocaine. While the ease of using China White makes it an attractive choice, it also makes it a dangerous one. It is easy to overdose on a drug so strong.

First-time heroin users often experience extreme vomiting and severe headaches. Some users regularly suffer diarrhea, muscle cramps, and stomach cramps. Most first-time users are told that the high will get better and the side effects will go away. And they usually try it enough to find out that what they were told was true. They also become addicted.

The use of heroin is increasing, especially among young people, because of the ease of using and widespread availability of China White. Although law enforcement officials can only estimate, they believe that there are about 2 million heroin users today, which is about four times as many users as five years ago.

Heroin is very addictive and destructive to your body and mind. Although it may take time, heroin will take your life over. It begins by numbing your mind and ends by destroying your body. You forget about eating or sleeping. You begin to waste away, focusing only on when you can get high. Most heroin addicts cannot hold a job or concentrate on one task for any length of time. They often turn to crime to help pay for their habit. Then they must deal not only with the effects of the drug on their bodies and minds, but with the result of their crimes.

Because heroin is often injected with a hypodermic needle, yet another risk in using heroin is acquiring the human immunodeficiency virus, or HIV, the virus believed to be one cause of AIDS, acquired immunodeficiency syndrome. It is essential for heroin users not to share needles. If that is unavoidable, it is vital that they wash the needle with bleach at least three times before using it.

It is possible to overcome an addiction to heroin. Check the Help List for resources.

# CHAPTER 4

# So How Do You Get Sleep?

*W*hether you suffer from insomnia, snoring, or self-induced sleep deprivation, there are general tips for getting a good night's sleep that do not include the use of chemical substances to induce sleep.

## General Tips

• Avoid caffeine and other stimulants completely. You may suffer withdrawal symptoms, including sluggishness, headaches, and daytime sleepiness, but they will not last longer than a week.
• Daily physical exercise will improve your night's sleep. It will also slightly

Regular exercise decreases the amount of sleep you need and improves the quality of the sleep you get.

decrease the amount of sleep you need. However, if you exercise within three hours before bedtime, your alertness will increase and you will have a difficult time falling asleep. The best time to exercise to induce restful sleep is between the hours of noon and 6 p.m.

• Take a power nap to counteract day-time sleepiness. Rather than reaching for a caffeinated soda, try to nap for 15 to 20 minutes during lunch if you feel tired during the day. According to Dr. James Maas at Cornell Uni-

52  versity, these power naps will increase your alertness, productivity,
and creativity. He cautions against
longer naps, however, because you
will awaken feeling groggy.

- Try to establish a regular sleeping
pattern. Going to sleep and waking
up at the same time every day (including weekends) helps your body
regulate itself. Cheating yourself out
of sleep during the week and trying
to make it up by sleeping late on the
weekends only confuses your body's
normal sleep-wake rhythm. The insomnia that most people feel on
Sunday nights by sleeping late on the
weekends is curable simply by to
sticking to an established sleep
schedule. If you have to get up at 6
a.m. during the week, and you need
eight hours of sleep, you should go
to bed at 10 p.m. every night. Your
body will get used to the schedule. If
you are well rested you shouldn't
need an alarm to wake up.

## Tips for People with Insomnia

- Definitely avoid caffeine. That
includes chocolate and all caffeinated

beverages. Read the labels to find out which sodas contain caffeine. A few labels might surprise you. Did you know that Sunkist Orange soda and Mountain Dew have caffeine? And did you know that root beer and cream soda do not?

- Try to avoid eating heavy foods such as potato chips, ice cream, cakes, or cookies before going to bed.
- A light snack, such as herbal tea, milk (warm or cold), yogurt, or a banana may help induce sleep.
- Take a hot bath before bed. It will relax your mind and muscles.
- Read a favorite book, magazine, or comic book until you feel sleepy enough to turn out the light.
- Write in a journal. Insomnia is usually caused by traumatic or anxiety-producing things happening in your life. Write about them. Write down worries, fears, thoughts, feelings, things to do, or story ideas. You will accomplish two things. First, you will free your mind for sleep. Second, you will have recorded things you need to, want to, or should deal with the next day.
- If you find that after 20 minutes you

54   are still tossing and turning, get up and do something else until you feel sleepy again. Watch TV, do a puzzle, or wash the dishes. Then go back to bed and try again.

Finally, if you find that you just can't sleep no matter what you do, talk to your doctor. He may be able to recommend other, stronger treatments.

### Snoring and Sleep Apnea

Try rolling over onto one side. Both snoring and sleep apnea occur most often when the sufferer is sleeping on his back. Rolling onto one side opens up the airway and makes breathing easier. The sleeper may never know the difference, but anyone sleeping in the same room will.

### Narcolepsy and Periodic Leg Movements Syndrome

There is little that one who suffers from either narcolepsy or periodic leg movements syndrome can do other than consult a doctor. A doctor can prescribe a treatment and might even recommend going to a sleep clinic. There they can study your case and advise the best method of dealing with the disorder.

# CHAPTER 5

# Dealing with Drug Addiction

*P*erhaps you're an occasional, or recreational, drug user. You've smoked a couple
of joints in your day, had a few beers,
tried a tab or two of acid with your
friends. Perhaps you also suffer from
some sort of sleeping disorder: You have
trouble falling asleep, you wake up a lot
during the night, or you just can't get up
in the morning. Now you know that some
of your problems sleeping might be re-
lated to your recreational drug use. You
might rightly draw the conclusion that, in
order to sleep better and have more pro-
ductive, less sleepy days, you should
avoid all drug use. That includes any occasional beers.

There are hundreds of things you can

*56* do that cost about the same or less than a hit of acid, a six-pack of beer, or a dime-bag of marijuana. Rent a movie, go bowling, take horseback riding lessons, sign up for an art class at a local museum, visit historic landmarks, learn a new craft, read a book, join the local theater, take up a sport or play intramural sports, join a club, volunteer as a Big Brother or Big Sister. None of these things will inhibit your sleep. In fact, many of them will enhance it.

Perhaps your use of drugs is more serious, to the point of addiction. You can't get through a day without taking a drink, or shooting up, or snorting, or popping a pill. You also suffer from sleeping disorders, but they are secondary to your big problem: addiction. You need to talk to someone you trust, an adult, a parent, a teacher, a guidance counselor, a priest, rabbi, or other religious leader.

Maybe you don't have anyone to turn to. There are several agencies established just to help people like you. They have toll-free numbers that you can call to talk about your problem. Many are also anonymous. They don't require any information about you. They only want to give you the information you need to get help.

Their numbers are listed in the back of this book.

Remember, it's never too late. You can always stop using drugs. Sometimes it is more difficult than others, but where there's a will, there's a way. Your life is worth the extra effort.

# Glossary
## Explaining New Words

**addiction**   Psychological or physical dependence on a drug.

**amphetamine**   Man-made drug used as a stimulant.

**barbiturate**   Man-made drug used as a sedative.

**caffeine**   Drug with stimulant quality found in coffee beans and tea leaves.

**insomnia**   Inability to sleep.

**narcolepsy**   Disorder inducing sleep attacks.

**NREM**   Non-REM sleep: Periods of sleep during which the eyes are still.

**over-the-counter**   Available without a prescription.

**prescription**   Medication whose use and purchase was advised by a doctor.

**psychoanalyst**   Doctor who treats mental illnesses by considering both the conscious and unconscious life of a patient.

**rejuvenate**   Give new life and vitality.

**REM**   Rapid eye movement: Period of sleep during which the eyes move rapidly as dreams occur.

**sedative**   Drug influence that induces calm or sleep.

**sleep apnea**   Disorder in which breathing temporarily stops during sleep.

**sleep deprivation**   Preventing from getting sleep.

**somnambulism**   Walking while sleeping.

**stimulant**   Substance that excites or arouses the body.

**tranquilizer**   Drug used to diminish anxiety.

# Help List

If you think you have a sleeping disorder, the best person to talk to is your doctor. Make a detailed list of all the symptoms you have (difficulty falling asleep, restless sleep, daytime sleepiness, etc.), and take them with you when you see the doctor. He may be able to recommend a course of treatment such as changing your bedtime, eliminating caffeine or other foods from your diet, or just making an effort to get more rest.

If the doctor suspects you have a serious sleeping disorder such as narcolepsy, he may also recommend that you go to a sleep clinic. Sleep clinics are set up to study a patient while he sleeps so that they can confirm the doctor's diagnosis. They and your doctor can then prescribe a course of treatment for you.

You might also try contacting the following organizations for more information about sleeping disorders.

**National Sleep Foundation**
122 South Robertson Boulevard
Los Angeles, CA 90048
1-310-288-0466

**Canadian Sleep Society**
500 Nassau Mills Drive
Peterborough, ON K9J 7B8

If you are suffering from drug or alcohol addiction, there are several places you can write to or call.

## Alcoholics Anonymous (AA)

This is a support group for alcoholics. There are branches of AA all over North America. Many also have a 24-hour hotline that you can call. Check the yellow pages for listings of a local meeting or hotline.

## Cocaine Anonymous (CA)

Like AA, there are branches all over North America. Check your local yellow pages for listings.

### Drug and Alcohol Hotline
1-212-874-6465

### Alcohol and Drug Dependency Information and Counseling Services (ADDICS)
#2, 2471 1/2 Portage Avenue
Winnipeg, NB R3J 0N6
204-831-1999

### Narcotics Anonymous
P.O. Box 7500, Station A
Toronto, ON M5W 1P9
416-691-9519

# For Further Reading

Borbely, Alexander. *Secrets of Sleep*. New York: Basic Books, Inc., 1986.

Buckalew, M. Walker. *Drugs and Stress*. New York: Rosen Publishing Group, 1993.

Dotto, Lydia. *Losing Sleep*. New York: William Morrow and Co., Inc., 1990.

Hales, Dianne. *The Complete Book of Sleep*. Reading, MA: Addison-Wesley Publishing Co., 1981.

Hauri, Peter, and Linde, Shirley. *No More Sleepless Nights*. New York: John Wiley and Sons, Inc., 1990.

Rawls, Bea O'Donnell, and Johnson, Gwen. *Drugs and Where to Turn*. New York: Rosen Publishing Group, 1993.

Simpson, Carolyn. *Coping with Sleep Disorders*. New York: Rosen Publishing Group, 1995.

# Index

**63**

## About the Author

Gina Strazzabosco-Hayn works as an editor and free-lance writer. She has written three books for young adults.

Ms. Strazzabosco-Hayn lives with her husband, Stephen, in New York.

## Photo Credits

Cover by Michael Brandt; pp. 2, 18, 28, 38, 44, 46, 51 by Kim Sonsky/Matthew Baumann; p. 35 by Yung-Hee Chia; all other photos by Kathleen McClancy.